# *Precious Moments with*
# GOD'S LITTLE ANGELS

### Written by Tami Glasper

Illustrations By Ruben Castaneda Jr.

*AuthorHouse™*
*1663 Liberty Drive*
*Bloomington, IN 47403*
*www.authorhouse.com*
*Phone: 1 (800) 839-8640*

*Published by AuthorHouse 01/18/2018*

*ISBN: 978-1-5462-2224-8 (sc)*
*ISBN: 978-1-5462-2225-5 (e)*

*Print information available on the last page.*

*Any people depicted in stock imagery provided by Thinkstock are models,*
*and such images are being used for illustrative purposes only.*
*Certain stock imagery © Thinkstock.*

*This book is printed on acid-free paper.*

*Because of the dynamic nature of the Internet, any web addresses or links contained in this book may have changed since publication and may no longer be valid. The views expressed in this work are solely those of the author and do not necessarily reflect the views of the publisher, and the publisher hereby disclaims any responsibility for them.*

authorHOUSE®

Ruben: This book is dedicated to Maria, Ruben III, and Jazmin.

Tami: This book is dedicated to Mark Sr, Mark Jr, Mya, and Matthew.

As a child of God,

I walk in dignity

Because my Father

cares

for me.

I live in

spiritual royalty.

2 Timothy 4:8
There is a crown of righteousness stored up for me.

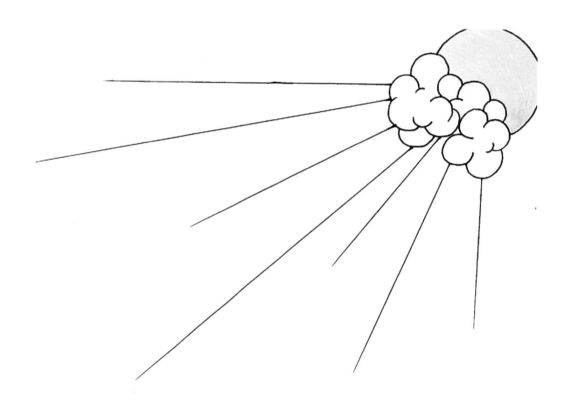

Matthew 5:16

Let your light shine

before men.


With the love of Jesus,

May I brighten someone's day

In the warmth of His love,

Jesus is the way

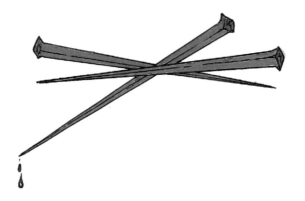

John 20:25

Jesus shows

disciples where nails

were in

his hands.


Through the pain of this world,

I will keep my eyes on Christ

He gave His life for mine

For my sins, Christ paid the price.

Proverbs 17:6

Grandchildren are like

crowns to grandparents

and children are

their parents' glory.


With humbleness in my

heart and on my head

a crown of grace.

In God's Holy Word,

may I walk in obedience.

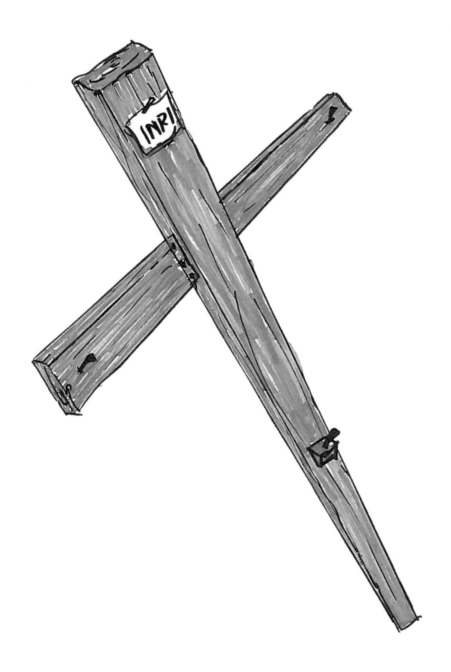

Mark 16:19

Jesus Christ was

received into

heaven.


God the Father, Son, and Holy

Spirit is the Trinity

We are saved by grace

through all eternity.

Matthew 6:21

Where my treasures are, there my heart will be.


I will keep focused on living a Godly life. My rewards are in heaven.

Matthew 18:3

Children are precious

in God's sight.


I walk in confidence of who I am.

I am a soldier in God's army, a follower of Jesus Christ.

Galatians 5:22-23

Fruit of the Spirit: love, joy, peace, patience,

kindness, goodness, faithfulness, gentleness, and self control.


Love, joy, peace be with you
today. Holy Spirit have
Your way. Praising God always.

John 8:7

He who is without sin

cast the first stone.


God's

children are sisters and brothers.

Not judging,

let us be kind to one

another.

Printed in the United States
By Bookmasters